First Facts®

FUN SCIENCE

Experiments in

FORCES AND MOTION

with Toys and Everyday Stuff

BY EMILY SOHN

T0060898

Consultant:
Paul Ohmann, PhD
Associate Professor of Physics
University of St. Thomas
St. Paul, Minnesota

CAPSTONE PRESS
a capstone imprint

First Facts are published by Capstone Press,
1710 Roe Crest Drive, North Mankato, Minnesota 56003
www.capstonepub.com

Library of Congress Cataloging-in-Publication Data
Sohn, Emily, author.
  Experiments in forces and motion with toys and everyday stuff / by Emily Sohn.
     pages cm—(First facts. Fun science)
  Includes bibliographical references and index.
  Summary: "Step-by-step instructions for experiments pertaining to forces, motion, and simple machines"—Provided by publisher.
  Audience: 5–8.
  Audience: K to 3.
  ISBN 978-1-4914-5032-1 (library binding)
  ISBN 978-1-4914-5072-7 (paperback)
  ISBN 978-1-4914-5076-5 (eBook PDF)
1. Force and energy—Experiments—Juvenile literature. 2. Motion—Experiments—Juvenile literature. 3. Simple machines—Experiments—Juvenile literature. 4. Toys—Juvenile literature.
I. Title. II. Series: First facts. Fun science.
  QC73.4.S646 2016
  531'.6078—dc23   2014048639

Editorial Credits
Alesha Sullivan, editor; Kyle Grenz, designer; Jo Miller, media researcher;
Kathy McColley, production specialist

Photo Credits
Capstone Studio/Karon Dubke except: Shutterstock: Nenov Brothers Images, cover (blocks), STILLFX, cover (marbles)

TABLE of CONTENTS

TURN YOUR HOME INTO A SCIENCE LAB!

Did you know your toys can teach you about why things move the way they do? **Forces** push and pull things to make them stop and go. Forces show up in all sorts of places—from space to the park to the game room. Get ready to have some fun with forces and **motion**!

force—any action that changes the movement of an object

motion—movement

Safety First!

You may need an adult's help for some of these experiments. But most of them can be done on your own. If you have a question about how to do a step safely, be sure to ask an adult. Think safety first!

FLIP TO PAGE 20 TO SEE HOW THE SCIENCE WORKS IN EACH EXPERIMENT!

MOVE IT!

Have you ever watched a racecar zoom by? Or have you spotted an airplane flying high up in the sky? These motions couldn't happen without forces. Check out a few ways to make your own toy car whiz forward!

Materials:

string

pencil

tape

toy car

Stay in Motion

An object that's resting will stay still unless a force makes it move. An object that's moving will keep moving until a force makes it stop. This is Newton's First Law of Motion. Isaac Newton was a **scientist**. He lived in England from 1643 to 1727.

Steps:

1. **Put a toy car on a flat surface. Use your finger to push it forward.**

2. **Push a pencil against the car to make the car go.**

3. **Use tape to attach a piece of string to the car. Pull the string to move the car.**

4. **Repeat steps 2 and 3 with the car turned upside down. Which way was easier? Can you think of other kinds of forces? How many ways can you move the car?**

scientist—a person who studies the world around us

STOP THAT TRUCK!

When an object is moving, ***frictional*** forces stop it. When you run down the sidewalk, you can stop because of the friction between your shoes and the ground. But what if you run down the sidewalk and want to stop in a puddle? Friction is still there, but there is less of it. Try playing with friction with some of your toys!

Materials:

toy truck

two building blocks

tape measure

friction—a force produced when two objects rub against each other; friction slows down objects

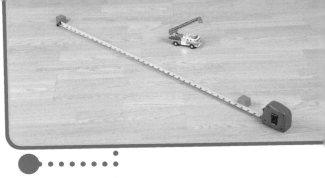

Steps:

1. Sit on a flat, hard floor. Measure a distance of 3 feet (1 meter). Use blocks to mark the start and finish lines.

2. Push the truck so it rolls from the start to the finish.

3. Measure 3 feet (1 m) outside in the grass. Use the blocks to mark the start and finish lines.

4. Push the truck so it rolls from the start to the finish. Was it harder to push the truck on the floor or the grass?

5. Try rolling the truck on a bumpy sidewalk or on gravel. Which surfaces have the most friction?

Fact:

Rub your hands together quickly. You will feel how friction can also cause heat.

9

WHAT GOES UP MUST COME DOWN

Why does a ball fall to the ground after you throw it? Because **gravity** is at work. Gravity is a type of force that makes things fall to Earth. Catch gravity in action with this simple activity!

Materials:

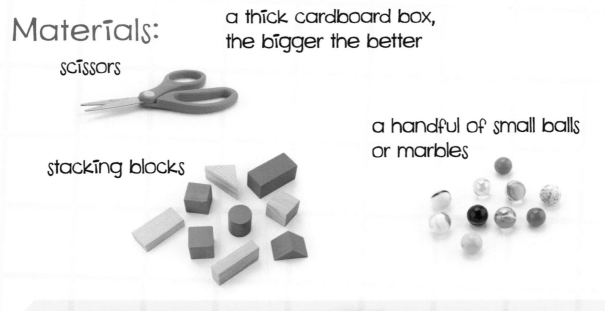

a thick cardboard box, the bigger the better

scissors

stacking blocks

a handful of small balls or marbles

gravity—a force that pulls objects with mass together; gravity pulls objects down toward the center of Earth

Steps:

1. **With an adult's help, cut long strips out of a box. Bend the strips so the edges are curved slightly. These are your ramps.**

2. **Use blocks to set up the ramps. Some will be steeper than others.**

3. **Let balls or marbles roll down each ramp. What direction do they roll?**

4. **Release two balls at the same time on two ramps. Have a race! Does one ball roll faster than the other?**

Fact:

Some planets have more gravity than others. The amount of gravity affects how much things weigh. If you weigh 55 pounds (25 kilograms) on Earth, you'd weigh 139 pounds (63 kg) on Jupiter. You'd weigh just 21 pounds (10 kg) on Mars. On the Sun, you'd weigh 1,540 pounds (699 kg)!

FIGHTING FORCES

Gravity pulls objects toward Earth.
Big, tall buildings are built to resist gravity.
Thick walls keep them from falling down.
Here's your chance to think like a builder
using some of your toys!

Materials:

interlocking toy bricks

Steps:

1. **Build a tower using interlocking toy bricks. How high can you make it before it tips over?**

2. **Try building a second tower with a thicker base. Did the tower fall over? Is it taller than the first tower? Does it fall over?**

3. **Keep adding bricks to make your tower as tall as you can. Can you think of other ways to fight gravity?**

TUG AWAY

More force produces more motion. If you lightly tap a soccer ball, it won't move very far. But if you kick the ball hard, it will travel farther. See for yourself in a game of tug-of-war. Prepare to pull as hard as you can!

Materials:

a friend or sibling

a rope or an old sheet twisted into a rope

an adult

Tip:
Have an adult supervise this activity.

Steps:

1. **Find a friend who is about the same size as you. Hold one end of the rope. Have your friend hold the other end. On the count of three, both of you should pull as hard as you can. Who won?**

2. **In the next match, use just one arm while your friend uses two arms. Try again using two arms while your friend uses only one. Did the results change? Who won the matches?**

3. **Now try playing against an adult. Did you win or lose?**

Weight Matters

Mass is the amount of material in an object. A person who weighs more than you do has more mass. An object with more mass needs more force to change its motion. Imagine running next to an adult. It would take more force to stop the adult than it would take for you to stop.

CRAZY BALLOONS

Large garbage trucks move forward. Skateboards can *curve* around a corner. Why do things move the way they do? In this activity, you can see how forces make objects move in all sorts of ways. Have a balloon race with a friend!

Materials:

a friend or sibling

balloons

curve—to bend or turn gently and continuously

Steps:

1. **Blow up a balloon. Have a friend do the same. Pinch the opening shut with your fingers.**

2. **Stand side-by-side with your friend, and let the balloons go. What happened to the balloons? Which balloon stayed in the air longer? Did they start out moving in the same direction?**

3. **Now face each other instead. Repeat Steps 1 and 2. Which way does each balloon fly? Did you notice how the balloon moved the opposite way that the air blew?**

Tip:

With more air, a balloon can fly farther.

LEVER POWER

Machines often produce force. Some machines are large, such as tractors. Other machines are smaller and simpler. A simple machine can even be a screw holding up a picture frame on the wall in your home. Try creating force in this easy experiment with a simple machine!

Materials:

a ruler

triangle-shaped block

heavy objects, like a book or a rock

machine—a piece of equipment that is used to do a job or make it easier to do something

18

Steps:

1. **Place a ruler on a block like a seesaw to make a *lever*.**

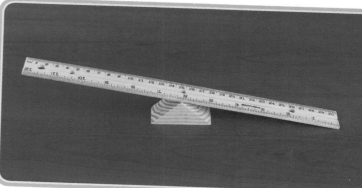

2. **Put a heavy object on one end of the lever. Push down on the other side.**

3. **Experiment with moving the block to change the position of the lever. How could you build a lever to lift even more weight? Could you make a lever strong enough to lift a person?**

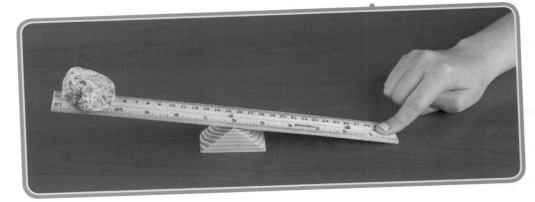

lever—a bar that turns on a resting point and is used to lift items

WHY IT WORKS

Are you wondering how these amazing experiments worked? Here is the science behind the fun!

PAGE 6 - MOVE IT!

To move a toy, you could push or pull it. You could blow on it, drop it, or kick it. There are many possible forces that can act on a toy or object.

PAGE 8 - STOP THAT TRUCK!

There is more friction on rough surfaces than on smooth surfaces. On a smooth surface, the truck moves easily. Outside, the grass rubs against the truck wheels, slowing the truck down. A truck pushed with the same force will move farther on a smooth floor than on dirt or grass.

PAGE 10 - WHAT GOES UP MUST COME DOWN

Gravity keeps the air around us and other objects from floating off into space. Gravity also makes objects fall to the ground. This pull is why the balls or marbles roll downward on the ramps. If the objects are the same size and mass, they will roll down the ramp at the same speed.

PAGE 12 - FIGHTING FORCES

Tall buildings need to be built the right way. Otherwise, gravity will pull them down! With a thicker base, the building is more **stable**, like the tower you built.

PAGE 14 - TUG AWAY

A person with more mass will usually be able to produce more force. Compared to a kid, a big adult will be able to pull harder and most likely win a game of tug-of-war.

PAGE 16 - CRAZY BALLOONS

When you let go of a balloon, look at which way the air is blowing out of it. The balloon will move in the opposite direction. Putting more air in the balloon will make it zoom through the air longer.

PAGE 18 - LEVER POWER

People have been using levers for thousands of years. Even your arm is a kind of lever! Less force is needed to lift something when a lever is used than if a lever isn't used. Levers and other types of machines make work easier for people.

stable—not easily moved

GLOSSARY

curve (KURV)—to bend or turn gently and continuously

force (FORS)—any action that changes the movement of an object

friction (FRIK-shuhn)—a force produced when two objects rub against each other; friction slows down objects

gravity (GRAV-uh-tee)—a force that pulls objects with mass together; gravity pulls objects down toward the center of Earth

lever (LEV-ur)—a bar that turns on a resting point and is used to lift items

machine (muh-SHEEN)—a piece of equipment that is used to do a job or make it easier to do something

mass (MASS)—the amount of material in an object

motion (MOH-shuhn)—movement

scientist (SYE-un-tist)—a person who studies the world around us

stable (STAY-buhl)—not easily moved

READ MORE

Biskup, Agnieszka. *The Gripping Truth About Forces and Motion.* LOL physical science. North Mankato, Minn.: Capstone Press, 2013.

Coupe, Robert. *Force and Motion.* How It Works. New York: PowerKids Press, 2014.

Oxlade, Chris. *Making Machines with Levers.* Simple Machine Projects. Chicago: Capstone Raintree, 2015.

INTERNET SITES

FactHound offers a safe, fun way to find Internet sites related to this book. All of the sites on FactHound have been researched by our staff.

Here's all you do:

Visit *www.facthound.com*

Type in this code: 9781491450321

Super-cool stuff! Check out projects, games and lots more at **www.capstonekids.com**

INDEX